# 2.19

Pub (*,, uuns*

in the

LAKE DISTRICT

Terry Marsh

• *25 circular walks including country inns* •

DALESMAN

Dalesman Publishing Company
Stable Courtyard, Broughton Hall,
Skipton, North Yorkshire BD23 3AE

First Edition 1997

Text © Terry Marsh
Illustrations © Geoff Cowton
Maps by Jeremy Ashcroft
Cover: Mortal Man, Troutbeck

A British Library Cataloguing in Publication record
is available for this book
ISBN 1 85568 111 0

Other books in this series:
Pub Walks in the Yorkshire Dales
by Richard Musgrave (ISBN 1 85568 103 X)
Pub Walks on the North York Moors and Coast
by Richard Musgrave (ISBN 185568 087 4)

Printed by Amadeus Press, Huddersfield

Pub Walks

in the

LAKE DISTRICT

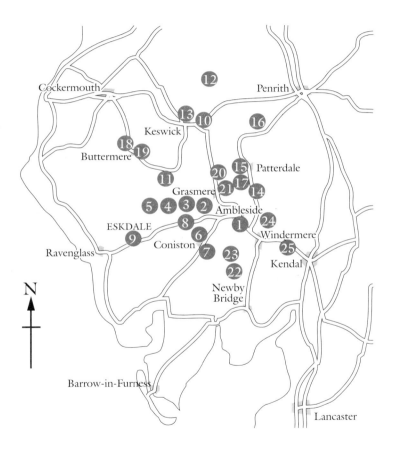

$\mathcal{W}$ALKS

INTRODUCTION

The present day image of an inn or pub, in which people sit around at tables having a drink or food in a convivial atmosphere, possibly while conducting business meetings, is far from modern. It probably dates from the Roman tabernae vinariae, though there is little doubt that many rural families were already diligently making alcoholic drinks from a range of ingredients – apples, pears, berries, honey and so on. By the time the Romans did arrive, from 43AD, the Britons were drinking a home-brewed ale, called curmi, produced from barley and other cereals brought to these islands by the sea-going Phoenicians from what is now Syria.

The Saxons, who followed the Romans, did much to encourage the drinking of ale, or îl, as they called it. Before long, those who brewed the best ales, usually the women, were busily selling it, at first to friends and neighbours, but later more widely. The Normans, who arrived in 1066, took their drinking very seriously, sufficiently so to regulate the production of ale. By the end of the 11th century the "ale house" had become a well-established haunt for many levels of society. Paradoxically, it was the religious houses and the monastic rules of hospitality that took the increase of ale drinking and travellers' "hospices" further, as the march of Christianity saw many inns, as they became known, developing under church or monastic control, in spite of a doctrine of temperance and moderation.

It was among much later travellers such as Dr Johnson, Daniel Defoe and Charles Dickens, however, that the "public house" – a Victorian appellation – became of key importance, and partly from their writings and enthusiasms that the inn became a much-celebrated part of the British way of life.

The differences between traditional terms like inn, pub, alehouse and tavern have progressively become more obscure, but in the past each of these held very clearly-defined responsibilities. Pubs, most of which were in villages, grew from the alehouses, and were smaller in scale than inns. Unlike a hotel, which is the modern version of an inn, not only offering food and drink to travellers but lodgings too, pubs did not provide accommodation until the 17th century. The tavern, on the other hand, differed from the alehouse only in what it supplied, namely wine rather than beer or ale.

All the pubs in this book have one thing in common; they welcome walkers. They also provide a wide selection of refreshments, as well as accommodation. As recreational walking continues its popularity as one of Britain's principal leisure pursuits, so the idea has evolved of doing comparatively easy walks that allow time to spend in the conviviality of rural pubs, perhaps rediscovering their significance as places of refuge for travellers, though it is to be hoped that no one tackling any of the 25 walks in this book will find themselves in need of a place of refuge.

All the proprietors were sent a questionnaire to ascertain that they would welcome walkers arriving in muddy boots and dripping wet from a day on the fells – not that such a condition is a prerequisite. But there seem to be a few too many pubs (and the clientele to go with them) that look askance at walkers in their midst, and the sooner all these remember their traditional origins, the better. Every proprietor has responded favourably, and many will allow walkers arriving by car to leave their vehicles on the pub car park, providing they ask permission first, and against the implied promise that they will avail themselves of the pub's hospitality on their return. Likewise, many pubs these days are happy to have children around the place and to cater for them – they are, after all, the next generation of pub walkers – and even to tolerate 'Fido', though for hygiene reasons he may have to be tied up outside.

Although there has been an assumption that most walkers will arrive by car and will then use the pubs from which the walks begin, there is no encouragement, implied or otherwise, to drink and drive; quite the contrary. Indeed, there is ample scope to undertake all of the walks in this book using public transport. And as the campaign against drinking and driving quite rightly mounts, and the many problems caused by excessive car use increase, there is even greater reason to look at more environmentally friendly ways of getting about.

In the Lake District there are many small-scale bus operators (as well as larger concerns) that run services into some of the more remote parts of the region, and these are sensibly timed to accommodate a day on the fells. The Mountain Goat is one such, travelling to many parts of the district, while the Coniston Rambler, for example, the Watendlath Wanderer and the Tarn Hows Tourer (though neither of these last two is needed for the walks in this book) do much the same on a more limited scale.

Information about public transport is readily available at all Tourist Information Centres, and you may just be surprised at how easy, and pleasurable, it is to travel around while someone else does the driving. It can also be exceptionally good value, especially if you buy a daily or weekly rover ticket.

GEOFF COWTON

A childhood spent in inner-city Bradford did little to prepare Geoffrey Cowton for the captivating beauty of the countryside. So the effect of a school geography trip involving a walk from Grassington to Malham was dramatic. He says: "The trip was literally an eye-opener for me, having come from a place where there were no fields and we had only a tiny garden. I loved all of it."

The result was a life-long love affair with beautiful scenery and now he spends as much time as possible roaming the Dales and the Lake District, gathering material for his distinctive paintings and drawings.

The finished works are produced at his Glendale Studio in King Cross, Halifax, working from on-the-spot sketches and meticulous notes backed up by location photographs.

Geoff Cowton has drawn all the pubs featured in this book and also those in the other Dalesman books of this series: Pub Walks in the Yorkshire Dales and Pub Walks on the North York Moors and Coast.

PUBLISHER'S NOTE

The information given in this book has been provided in good faith and is intended only as a general guide. Whilst all reasonable efforts have been made to ensure that details were correct at the time of publication, the author and Dalesman Publishing Company Ltd cannot accept any responsibility for inaccuracies. It is the responsibility of individuals undertaking outdoor activities to approach the activity with caution and, especially if inexperienced, to do so under appropriate supervision. They should also carry the appropriate equipment and maps, be properly clothed and have adequate footwear. The sport described in this book is strenuous and individuals should ensure that they are suitably fit before embarking upon it.

GOLDEN RULE

This popular walk to Stockghyll Force is extended to include the summit of Wansfell, a steep but rewarding experience, and then runs down to idyllic Troutbeck.

DISTANCE:
6¼ miles
(10km)
WALKING
TIME:
3½-4 hours
MAP:
OS Outdoor
Leisure Map 7
TERRAIN:
Good paths
throughout, but
a steep pull to
Wansfell.
PARKING:
Main Ambleside
car park.

The Golden Rule lies tucked away up Smithy Brow, directly opposite the pedestrian entrance to the Ambleside car park. Here you can be sure of a friendly welcome, even if your boots are muddy or your waterproofs dripping. There is a back yard with tables and a small and attractive garden. The Golden Rule is a brass measuring yard mounted over the bar counter. Limited bar meals (snacks); children and dogs welcome. Tel 015394 33363.

Ambleside is a well-blessed centre for walkers, with days out ranging from a circuit of the mighty Fairfield Horseshoe to the joys of elevation that come from tackling Loughrigg Fell, or, as described here, Wansfell Pike. Unlike its nearby companions, Wansfell Pike provides a stunning view down the length of Windermere which alone justifies a visit to this rather lowly summit.

Although there are a number of car parks in Ambleside and some limited roadside parking, the main car park at the northern edge of the town is

11

the most sensible place to head for. Leave it by a
pedestrian footbridge, noting Smithy Brow slightly to the
left, where you will find the Golden Rule. Turn right into
the centre of town, and go past the Salutation Hotel,
leaving the main road here for a narrow road between
buildings to reach a back lane (signposted Waterfalls,
Stockghyll and Wansfell Pike). Before long you have the
chance to divert into Stockghyll Park to view the splendid
Stockghyll Force. The falls are at the highest point of the
park, so keep following the footpaths to and beyond a
viewing point, but do not cross the uppermost
footbridge. From the top falls, retrace your steps
a little then branch left on a path that leads
out to a large turnstile. Beyond the
turnstile you meet the lane you
left earlier. Turn left and

press on to cross a cattle grid.

Not long after the cattle grid, cross an arrangement of stiles on the right to enter a field. An ongoing footpath pursues the course of a beck, climbing easily up the field to another ladder stile at the end of an old track. Step across the track and through a wall gap, still following the beck as the path, renovated and waymarked in places, continues its ascent. Cross the beck by a small footbridge, then cross a wall before finally scampering up to the summit. The section between the old track and the top of the fell is quite steep, so take it easy, stopping frequently to admire the retrospective view across Ambleside of the Coniston and Langdale Fells.

The way now continues over the ridge to Troutbeck, setting off east across a fence, and down a clear path (slightly left) that runs down and round to a gate, and on again to the walled Nanny Lane. Now turn right and follow Nanny Lane to reach the Troutbeck road at Lane Foot Farm. Turn right on the road to the post office.

On the way keep your eyes open for a couple of drinking troughs set in the right hand wall. These are relics from the coaching days when the road you are walking was the main approach to the Kirkstone Pass and Patterdale beyond.

Just beyond the post office, leave the road for a track, Robin Lane (signposted Skelghyll, Jenkin Crag and Ambleside). Robin Lane rises gently for a while, and where it branches right at Hundreds Road, take the level path left through a gate for High Skelghyll, gradually descending to reach a metalled drive.

Go right and follow it to High Skelghyll, and continue

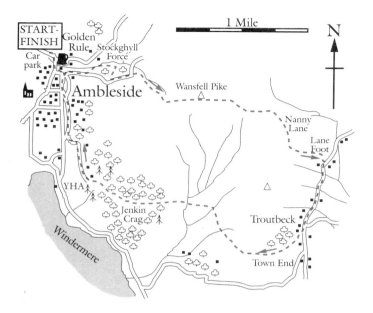

past the farmhouse through gates. Walk along the stony track that follows until eventually you enter Skelghyll Wood. A brief deviation to take in the celebrated view from Jenkin Crag is well worthwhile.

Back on the woodland path, go right at a fork and zigzag down to a bridge over Stencher Beck. The main track, ignoring a branching track on the left, continues down and leaves the wood to join an access lane, eventually merging into Old Lake Lane. Go right, to return to Ambleside by a less busy route than the parallel A591, which eventually it is forced to join. Keep going through the town centre then branch right up Smithy Brow to well-earned refreshment at the Golden Rule.

BRITANNIA INN

This delightful and easy walk meanders through farm fields and beside tarns, streams and rivers, with exquisite views of the surrounding fells.

DISTANCE:
5½ miles (9km)
WALKING
TIME: 3 hours
MAP: OS
Outdoor Leisure
Map 7
TERRAIN:
Good paths all
the way.
PARKING:
Elterwater car
park, just south
of the Britannia
Inn, or
Elterwater
Common, north
of the village.

Enormously popular with walkers, the Britannia Inn is everything you would expect of a traditional British inn. Painted black and white with colourful window boxes, the inn stands next to the village green and an ancient maple tree. Garden chairs and tables in a terraced forecourt are ideal for a post-perambulatory pick-me-up. Bar meals are served from 12 noon-5.30pm and 6.30-9.30pm. Children are very welcome, as are dogs (in the bars and bedrooms). Tel 015394 37210.

Start from the car park (note that because there is no roadside parking, you may have to park on Elterwater Common a short distance to the north of the village). Take the signposted path to Skelwith Bridge, which requires little in the way of description as it wanders on very pleasantly to a superb resting place beside Elter Water.

The Langdale Pikes rise across the tarn, their crags and gullies often so vividly etched you feel you could reach out and touch them.

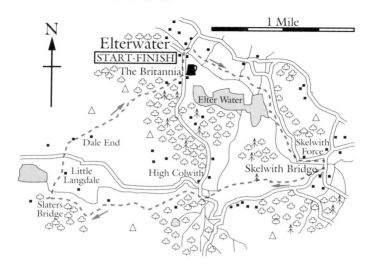

Beyond the tarn keep on, often quite close to the main road but sheltered from it by a wall, until you enter the site of the Kirkstone Quarry, not far from Skelwith Bridge (pronounced Skellyth).

The river flowing from Elter Water is the Brathay, which, just above Skelwith Bridge, produces Skelwith Force, an engaging cascade of foaming water in rich, green woods, and sheltered glades dappled by sunlight. This is a truly mesmeric spot, where good intentions can often be waylaid.

Beyond the works buildings, which barely detract from the walk, the track runs on to reach a small picnic site close by Skelwith Bridge, a delightful spot but too close to the busy and noisy Ambleside-Coniston road for peaceful enjoyment of your surroundings. So, turn right across the bridge and follow the road round a bend and uphill for a short distance as far as a signposted track for Colwith Bridge, on the right. Do take great care on this road, especially on the bend, keeping children under very close control; thankfully you only have to contend with it for a few minutes.

Having abandoned the road, a series of gates guides you along an obvious and most pleasant path, passing a few static caravans, until you reach Park Farm. The route (waymarked) lies between farm buildings (look for an apprentice stonemason's handiwork set in one wall), and continues through delightful nooks and crannies, gates and stiles until finally it debouches on to a lane.

Turn right for a few paces then, before a bridge, leave the

lane on the left for a signposted path for High Park and Colwith Force.

Bear right on a permissive path, and with little effort you rise to a viewpoint overlooking Colwith Force, a waterfall that is rather shy about proclaiming its undoubted attractions. With the river (still the Brathay, flowing from Little Langdale Tarn and into Elter Water) always on your right, keep going across more fields until finally you reach High Park Farm. Turn left and rise to a cattle grid at a lane, turning right down the lane to reach Stang End, where the road neatly nips around the buildings.

Stay on this quiet lane until in due course you reach the edge of woodland and can follow a broad track round to a footbridge spanning the shallow Brathay. Do not cross the bridge, but instead go left beside the river on a rough track until, at a kissing gate on the right, you can leave the track to approach Slater's Bridge, a superb legacy of past quarrying times.

Cross the bridge and keep straight ahead beside a wall on your right (ignoring gaps and diverting pathways). The path rises a little with the wall, with an outstanding view to your left of Little Langdale Tarn and Greenburndale beyond. The path leads up to a farm access, where you turn left and follow it to the Little Langdale road.

Left again and immediately right brings you on to another lane that after another farm degenerates into a stony track and takes you on down, strolling delightfully for quite some time until regrettably you reach the road leading left, back into Elterwater.

WAINWRIGHT'S INN

C H A P E L   S T I L E

An easy walk making use of a section of the Cumbria Way, in the hope of tempting some walkers into a longer exploration of the Lakes.

DISTANCE: 3³/₄ miles (6km)
WALKING TIME: 2 hours
MAP: OS Outdoor Leisure Map 6
TERRAIN: Easy walking on good paths.
PARKING: Wainwright's Inn (ask permission first).

This homely inn offers a relaxed and friendly atmosphere in its spacious slate-floored bar. It is in a delightful spot for exploring adjoining fells around Chapel Stile. Children and dogs are welcome, and bar meals are served from 12 noon-2pm (2.30pm on Sundays) and 6-9.30pm. Tel 015394 38092.

Just past Wainwright's Inn heading towards Chapel Stile, a signposted footpath leads away from the road and on to a surfaced lane that goes past Thrang Farm and through a gate. Beyond the gate the lane becomes a path. Keep on to another gate and through this to a junction with a track on the edge of the village of Chapel Stile.

Over the years the village grew as it became the home of generations of quarrymen who worked the surrounding fellsides.

Bear left along the track to a bridge spanning Great Langdale Beck.

Turn right (you are now on the Cumbria Way) and, with the river on

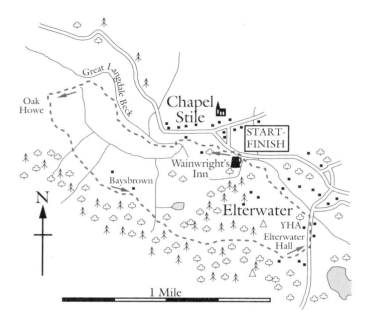

your right, follow the track across several fields until it finally trends away from the river to a gate. Through the gate follow the track round to Oak Howe cottage and keep left by a wall past a barn to cross a stream.

Along Great Langdale Beck you may have noticed how the banks have been consolidated as a measure against the flooding which used to occur from time to time. Indeed, many years ago this area would have resembled the marshy region around Elter Water.

Over the stream go left on a stony path that is often wet and slippery, to reach a gate. Keep going with a wall on your left, past a sheep enclosure, to a gate. Maintain the same direction through oak woodland to reach another surfaced lane.

The woodland would have been used centuries ago to provide tannin to supply the leather industry, probably in industrial Lancashire, or to produce a timber crop.

Go left down the lane to Baysbrown Farm, and press on through a gate and along the lane to a junction where you can turn left to a T-junction. Another left turn takes you down to Elterwater.

As you approach Elterwater and before crossing the bridge over Great Langdale Beck, turn left up a lane with the river to your right. Keep on along the lane climbing

easily for a few hundred m/yds until you reach a descending footpath on the right, marked by a large stone sign, that leads to the river.

Go past slate spoil heaps and on towards a footbridge. Over the bridge you reach the main road only a short distance from Wainwright's Inn. Turn left to return to the start of the walk.

STICKLEBARN TAVERN

L A N G D A L E

𝒯his lazy low-level circuit of the Langdale valley still manages to gain enough height to afford an excellent view of the Pikes.

DISTANCE:
4 miles (6km)
WALKING TIME:
2 hours
MAP: OS Outdoor Leisure Map 6
TERRAIN:
Goods paths, but often stony.
PARKING:
National Trust car park immediately adjoining the Sticklebarn. Pay and display.

Originally a barn on a working farm, the Sticklebarn Tavern was developed about 25 years ago into a popular walkers' bar, with a terrace and picnic tables. Walkers will receive a warm welcome here, as will children and dogs. Bar meals are generally served from 12 noon-2.30pm and 6-9.30pm, but unbroken in the day during school holidays. There are some variations at weekends, so if this is important, call first. Tel 015394 37356.

Leave by the top end of the car park, jinking through a couple of gates as if taking the path that goes up to Stickle Tarn. When the path goes through a gap and then forks, keep left (ignoring the Stickle Tarn path) and ascend ahead to another gate on the immediate skyline. Beyond that the path wanders along the base of Raven Crag and Gimmer Crag, popular playgrounds for rock climbers who if they are present may provide you with free entertainment as you pass.

With little scope for getting lost, the

path guides you onwards to the Old Dungeon Ghyll
Hotel at the entrance to Mickleden. You reach it at the
start (by a gate) of the track into Mickleden, but, unless
you want two pubs for the price of one, ignore it and
follow a narrow path, keeping the hotel on your left, that
goes down to Middle Fell Farm and out to the valley
road. Turn right and then immediately left, as if heading
for unseen Blea Tarn beyond the cone of Side Pike.

A short way on at a bend, leave the road and enter the
nearby campsite, walking straight ahead through the
campsite until you can leave it at the rear by two step
stiles that bring you on to open pasture at the foot of
Side Pike. Now go left across pastures on an
improving path that eventually leads you

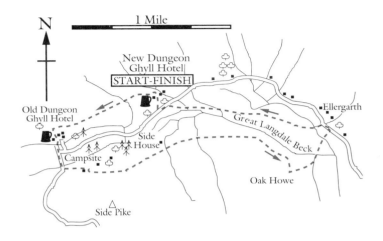

to meet the Cumbria Way near Side House Farm.

Keep the farm on your left (do not go towards it), pressing on up rising ground on a stony path that leads around the northern edge of Lingmoor Fell, with excellent retrospective views of the Langdale Pikes. The path is clear throughout and brings you easily to Oak Howe Farm. Branch left past the farm following a broad track, and then leave it, left, to reach a footbridge spanning Great Langdale Beck.

Cross the bridge and walk up to the valley road. Turn left along the road for 100m/yds, and then leave it, left, for a hedgerowed track (signposted) across pastures, that brings you out on the valley road once more near the National Park car park at New Dungeon Ghyll. Walk past the car park for a short distance, and turn right into the National Trust car park adjoining Sticklebarn Tavern.

OLD DUNGEON GHYLL

L A N G D A L E

A taste of the Cumbria Way and a couple of mountain passes feature in this walk at the western end of Great Langdale.

DISTANCE:
6 miles (10 km)
WALKING
TIME:
3-4 hours
MAP: OS
Outdoor Leisure
Map 6
TERRAIN:
Clear paths , but
boots and basic
hill-walking gear
needed. Not
advised in poor
visibility.
PARKING: Old
Dungeon Ghyll
(Limited; ask
permission first),
or nearby
National Trust
pay and display

For over 100 years the 'ODG' has offered a base for walkers and climbers. It was originally a farm and an inn run by a well-known tourist guide, John Bennett. In 1949, the shippon was converted into a climbers' bar, following which many of the climbing clubs in the country came to the ODG for their annual dinners. This meant that the best British climbers, some of whom had taken part in Everest and other Himalayan expeditions, stayed at the hotel. When the climbers' bar is full today you can be sure of a boisterous and friendly atmosphere. Bar meals are served from 12 noon-2pm and 6-9pm. Dogs and children are welcome. Tel 015394 37272.

Walk round the back of the hotel to start along the broad track that leads into the long valley of Mickleden, the northerly arm of the upper section of the Langdale valley.

You are here on the Cumbria Way, one of Lakeland's finest middle distance walks, which never strays far from and eventually runs quite close to

Mickleden Beck, an agreeable companion if you don't already have one with you! Ahead and slightly left, Bow Fell, one of the higher Lakeland fells, rises above the valley, its left skyline running down into The Band, the most popular way of ascent.

After about two miles you reach the foot of the Stake Pass, an ancient thoroughfare into Borrowdale to the north, probably dating from the thirteenth century and possibly earlier. Here branch right and ascend, steeply for a while, until you reach easier gradients in Langdale Combe. The top of the pass, with its views forward of the Borrowdale heights, is marked by a large cairn and a small tarn, though the tarn sometimes dries up. From here turn left on a clear path that leads you across the northern slopes of Rossett Pike to reach

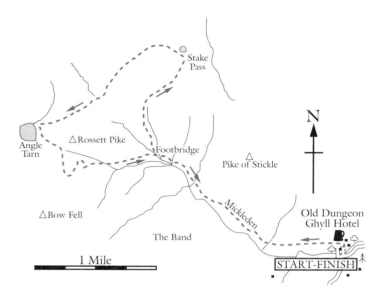

Angle Tarn, a beautiful dark-eyed lake set against the impressive backdrop of Esk Pike.

From the tarn, head south-east (left) and follow a well-trodden path to the top of Rossett Gill. If you wish you can make an optional ascent of nearby Rossett Pike by leaving the path on the left and climbing rough ground to the summit. In spite of its relatively modest elevation, Rossett Pike is a splendid coign of vantage for viewing the Langdale Pikes and their valley.

For many years Rossett Gill had a reputation for being one of the most laborious ascents and trying descents in Lakeland; it was frequently loose and awkward in places and unavoidable if bound for the Scafells from Langdale.

Some of those conditions still remain, but footpath improvements have eased the rigours of ascent and made the descent considerably less knee-jarring.

Launch yourself into the top of the gill, being especially careful if you have to negotiate loose rock. When you can deviate right from the main line of descent, do so. This is not essential, but it is more considerate of the need to minimise erosion, and you will find it a much easier proposition underfoot.

At the base of the gill all the difficulties such as they are, cease, and you continue down a rough and stony track to meet your outward route at the foot of the Stake Pass, from where you simply retrace your steps to the welcome of the Old Dungeon Ghyll.

THE SUN HOTEL

C O N I S T O N

This gentle walk follows the green paths formerly used by miners during the heyday of copper and slate mining among these Coniston Fells.

DISTANCE:
5 1/2 miles (9km)
WALKING
TIME: 3 hours
MAP: OS
Outdoor Leisure
Map 6
TERRAIN:
Mostly open,
bracken-clad
fellsides; not
suitable in poor
visibility.
PARKING: The
Sun Hotel (ask
permission
first), or you can
start from the
main Coniston
car park.

The Sun Hotel, tucked out of sight up a side lane from the bridge in the centre of Coniston, belies its apparent size, for inside you will find it reaches far back on both sides of the bar. Low, 17th-century black oak beams and lots of brasses lend character to this delightful inn. There is a separate area for walkers; and children are welcome, as are dogs. Bar meals are served from 12 noon-2pm and 6-9pm. Tel 015394 41248.

Whether you start from the Sun Hotel or the main car park, you need to walk to the bridge in the centre of Coniston and turn towards Ambleside.

Coniston is a lively and lovely place; many of its grey stone houses still have the round chimney stacks so characteristic of Lakeland homes. Tourism brought Coniston's wealth, as it still does, founded on the love for the area expressed by one man, John Ruskin, who lived and died in the shadow of the high fells that gather at Coniston's door.

Once part of Lancashire, Coniston is

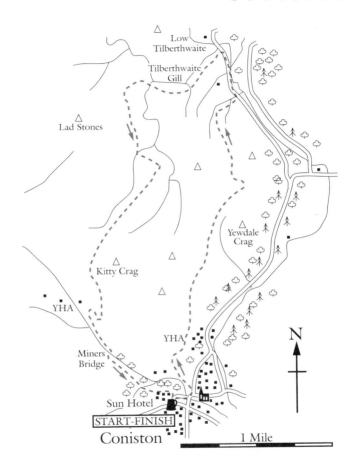

now wholly within Cumbria, and the once proud County summit, the Old Man, relegated to the also-rans among the greater group of Lakeland fells. Even so, the magnetism of this charming village grows stronger by the day, and *many among those who come to Coniston count it as a firm favourite.*

Walk along the main road for a few strides to a lane on the left beside the Black Bull. Go along this lane, and when the surfaced section ends go right, over a stile, on to a green path.

Keep on as far as a wooden gate and turn left on to a path through bracken, with improving views over Coniston Water and the Yewdale Fells as you climb. The path continues through gorse until you join a small stream leading to a tiny tarn. Cross the beck at the tarn's outflow, and look along the tarn for a cairn in a notch on the skyline. Head for this, and from it go down the right-

hand side of a grassy gully to another cairn at the bottom. Cross the gully, left, on to a vague path, and soon descend, right, to cross a stream, circling left round wet ground to another grassy gully with a cairn at the top. This gives you an especially fine view over the boggy expanse of Yewdale Moss.

Go down into a dip from which cairns define a path to a grassy ledge. Turn left on a higher path, and turn right at a cairn to take the right-hand of three paths that suddenly materialise. Now go downhill once more through bracken, with the path, indistinct at first, improving as you go.

When you arrive at the head of a gill, go left to reach a stone-edged track opposite. Ignore the path going down into the gill, which only leads to a quarry. Instead, go down the stone-edged path through crags to bend right following a stream to a path on the left.

Turn left and cross a stream, then climb to a col, where you pass through the remains of a wall. Now descend again, flanked by bracken to a small quarry hut. Turn left past a larger building and a tunnel into underground workings, but they are dangerous so please do not go in.

Stay on the main track, keeping on down to join the Tilberthwaite road. Turn left as far as the Tilberthwaite car park, on the edge of which take a path climbing up spoil past the entrances to Penny Rigg quarries and up to the ruins of a hut, beyond which you follow the rim of Tilberthwaite Gill. The path narrows and is a little awkward in one or two places for a moment, especially as it negotiates a side stream. The path eventually brings you out above the Tilberthwaite Gorge to a cairn at Crook Beck. Do not cross the beck but go left, following its cairned right bank.

Cross a stream above a rowan-flanked waterfall and then climb steadily on a clear path that rises to the reedy tarn at Hole Rake, the top of the pass, with a stunning view of the Old Man of Coniston directly ahead. The ongoing path bears left and goes down in zigzags to the rear of a group of four miners' cottages known as Irish Row. Keep left to reach the main valley track, and shortly right to cross Church Beck by a bridge, then pressing on down a clear track until you emerge beside the Sun Hotel.

BLACK BULL INN

C O N I S T O N

The oldest building in Coniston is visited on this easy walk, which then meanders along the shore of Coniston Water.

DISTANCE: 5¹/₂miles (9km)
WALKING TIME: 3 hours
MAP: OS Outdoor Leisure Map 6
TERRAIN: Well-signposted paths and tracks, with a few small unbridged streams.
PARKING: Main car park in Coniston. You can also park at the Black Bull (ask permission first).

The Black Bull Inn stands beside the main road into Coniston, and was built about the time of the Spanish Armada as a coaching inn to provide accommodation and refreshments for travellers, coachmen and horses. Its spacious black-beamed bar boasts an open fire that may well have been enjoyed by visitors such as Ruskin, de Quincey, Coleridge and the landscape artist Turner, all of whom visited or lived in the area. The Black Bull was also used as a venue during the filming of "Across the Lake", the film depicting the last 60 days of the life of Donald Campbell, who died on Coniston Water during his ill-fated attempt at the water speed record in 1967. Bar meals are served every day of the year from 12 noon-9pm. Separate area for walkers; dogs and children are welcome here. Tel 015394 41335/41668.

From the car park turn left and walk through the village, bearing left over the bridge next to the Black Bull, and going left past a petrol station, to the next turning on the left (signposted Gondola). Follow this road for about a quarter of a mile until the road turns sharply left. Now cross the road to a step stile (signpost), and turn right along a grassy path beside a hedgerow, to a gate. The path leads on with a fence on the left to a broad track heading for Coniston Hall.

Coniston Hall was built by the Fleming family in the fifteenth century, and there is evidence to suggest that the hall stands on the site of an earlier building from the time when the family gained Coniston by marriage in 1250.

Follow signposts through the grounds of Coniston Hall to a campsite, where you take the first track on the left which leads you down to the lakeshore. From a gate in a wall you look out on to a lush green field. This is the site of the Coniston bloomery, used for the smelting of iron ore from medieval

times until the 17th century.

Keep on along the lakeshore to a step stile which gives access to another campsite, and stay with a waymarked path, passing a slipway, and on to a track heading into Torver Common Wood. Stay with the track in the wood, never far from the lake, and cross a small stream after a short while to reach a sign directing you left on a path to a clearing, where there is a signpost for Torver.

Turn right, on a broad path across a vehicle track to go through a collapsed wall, after which the path becomes enclosed by trees and climbs to a gate and signpost. Go through the gate to a track leading to another gate beside a barn. Beyond the barn follow an enclosed track onwards to a stile, after which you turn right through a gate, then follow the line of a hedgerow to cross four gated fields. At the fifth field, head to a wall corner and follow the wall, right, to a nearby gap stile. After the stile, the path runs on through a pine plantation to a pasture. Cross a fence and turn right along the edge of woodland at the rear of Hoathwaite Farm.

The path now takes you through sheep pens to the farmyard. Turn left out of the farm and at its entrance go through a gate on your right into a camping site. Go across the top of the field, keeping a fence on your left, and pass a cattle grid to a grass track descending to a stream and a gate into a larch plantation. Stay with the track beside the stream to a stile and then cross the stream on stepping stones.

The way ahead keeps to an occasionally indistinct grassy track, bearing left to follow the base of rising ground to a

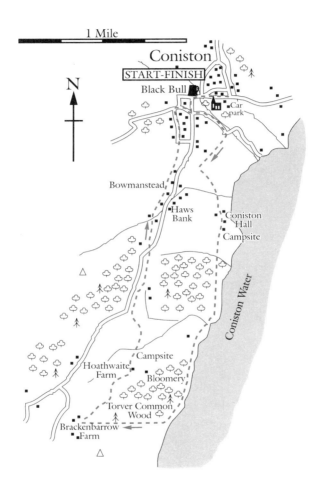

1 Mile

Coniston

START-FINISH

Black Bull

Car park

N

Bowmanstead

Haws Bank

Coniston Hall Campsite

Coniston Water

Campsite

Hoathwaite Farm

Bloomery

Torver Common Wood

Brackenbarrow Farm

gate in a wall. The gate gives access to the old Furness railway trackbed, which originally opened for the more efficient transportation of copper ore and slate, but from 1859 was instrumental in developing the wave of tourism then just beginning.

Through the gate turn right over a stile and follow a waymarked route past a caravan site, eventually reaching a narrow road. Follow the road for about 100m/yds until it bends sharply left, then locate a signposted track on the left taking you back on to the old railway trackbed. You can now follow the old railway line back to Coniston, which it reaches through a small modern housing estate on the site of the former Coniston railway station. Keep ahead to a T-junction, turn right and shortly left to go down past the Sun Hotel on a lane that brings you back into the village at Church Bridge and the Black Bull.

THREE SHIRES INN

L I T T L E   L A N G D A L E

This stunning little walk seems obvious from the map, yet you won't find it overcrowded even in summer.

DISTANCE:
5 miles (8km)
WALKING
TIME: 3 hours
MAP: OS
Outdoor Leisure
Map 6
TERRAIN:
Easy walking on
good paths. One
steepish pull
halfway round.
Walking boots
and equipment
are essential; not
advised in poor
visibility.
PARKING:
Three Shires Inn
(at quiet times;
please ask first,
an alternative
may be
suggested).

The "three shires" are the former counties of Cumberland, Lancashire and Westmorland that used to meet at the top of the Wrynose Pass, where you will still find the Three Shire Stone. The inn of that name is a delightful place (no smoking), with a comfortably extended back bar sporting antique oak carved settles. Bar meals and snacks are served every lunchtime and evening (except evenings in December and January, and Christmas Day). Children are welcome and well catered for with an adjoining natural garden and stream; dogs are welcome in the bar area. Tel 015394 37215.

From the inn, turn up the road for a short distance and then left (signposted Tilberthwaite), descending to a lane that leads past cottages and on to a rough track with a raised pedestrian walkway on the right. This leads to a footbridge over the River Brathay, beyond which you keep ahead to enter Atkinson Coppice.

At a junction of tracks bear right

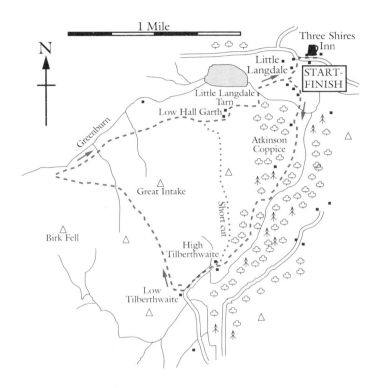

beside a wall and shortly enter Tilberthwaite Wood. At another fork bear right again (still signposted for Tilberthwaite).

Ascend easily through derelict quarry workings that Nature is gradually reclaiming, and keep ahead to a kissing gate and large six-bar gate. Keep on along the ensuing track to reach High Tilberthwaite Farm.

Just as you reach the farm, a path branches right to reach

a rising, stony track across the fells into Little Langdale, where it will eventually intercept the main track into Greenburndale. Use this only if you require a short cut, or you cannot face the climb from Low Tilberthwaite.

Go through the farm, leaving gates as you find them, and along the lane that leads down to Low Tilberthwaite. As you reach the cottages at Low Tilberthwaite swing right in front of them (note the spinning gallery at the first cottage), and follow a broad track as it bends upwards. Just before crossing a ravine, branch right on an indistinct, but improving grassy path rising steeply and head for a stile just visible in a barred wall gap above.

Over the stile climb beside a wall through bracken to reach a boggy plateau, quite unsuspected from below. Press on alongside the wall to some wooden enclosures for sheep. Cross a step stile over a fence, and rise with a narrow path towards a tall ladder stile, from where there is a stunning and sudden view of the Langdale Pikes.

Do not cross the stile but keep ahead, following the wall on your right. It descends steadily, and steeply at times, and crosses a side stream near another stile. Ignore this stile too, and keep going down beside the wall to reach the main track into Greenburndale.

Turn right and follow the track out of the valley, joined a short way on by the short cut mentioned earlier. Keep left here and go on past farm buildings and Low Hall Garth until you reach a kissing gate on the left, beyond which you can cross the attractive Slater's Bridge, constructed many years ago by men working at the quarries in Greenburndale.

Once across the bridge turn right through a wall gap, keeping ahead and rising below rock outcrops to another gate at a fence junction. Beyond this a path leads down to a gate giving access to the lane used at the start of the walk. Turn left to a junction, and then right, back to the Three Shires Inn.

BURNMOOR INN

BURNMOOR TARN & EEL TARN

For a walk on the wild side, there is little to better an exploration of the moors south of the main Scafell massif.

DISTANCE: 7 miles (11km)
WALKING TIME: 3-4 hours
MAP: OS Outdoor Leisure Map 6
TERRAIN: Pathways throughout, but many are indistinct, making this an inadvisable walk in misty conditions.
PARKING: Burnmoor Inn, Boot (ask permission first)

The Burnmoor Inn lies in a quiet part of the Lake District; you could easily miss Boot as you drive along the valley road. The inn is partly 16th century and is surrounded by peaceful fells in a region once inhabited by Bronze Age man, as stone circles on Boat How and elsewhere testify. Bar meals are served every day from 12 noon-2pm and 6-9pm. Children are welcome, but no dogs, please. Tel 019467 23224.

The walk begins from the once - industrial village of Boot, where the former corn mill is now the museum, and the ever-popular Eskdale to Ravenglass Railway is a narrow gauge railway that once served an iron mine.

Go over the stone-arched bridge and past the mill, following an ascending and stony bridleway towards Brat's Hill. The route zigzags a little to begin with, flanked by walls made of Eskdale granite. As you reach the wide expanse of Eskdale Moor, you encounter a group of derelict stone buildings that may well have served as peat houses, in which peat from the moor was dried and stored. As you pass the last building, walk out on to Brat's Moss heading for a now conspicuous grassy mound near Brat's Hill that conceals a stone circle, composed of some collapsed and standing stones, and within which five burial chambers have been discovered.

Ahead the path goes on to Low Longrigg, where there are more stone circles, though none of these contained human remains. The route then goes along the easy shoulder to Boat How, a small grassy summit with a rare view into Miterdale. A more obvious grassy path passes along the southern flank of Boat How, and you can use this if you wish.

BURNMOOR TARN & EEL TARN

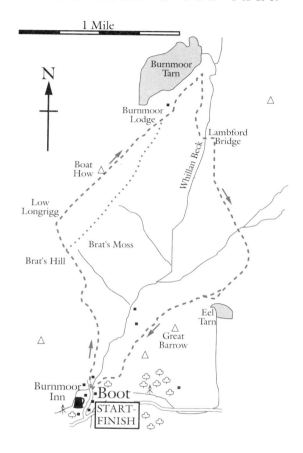

An easy descent now leads towards Burnmoor Tarn, one of the largest tarns in Lakeland, and Burnmoor Lodge, the latter indicating that the area was used by sporting parties, a fact confirmed by a line of shooting butts.

Burnmoor Tarn lies in a wide hollow crossed by an old

corpse road, and in spite of surrounding bogginess, it is an evocative place, where the call and flight of moorland birds give the wide open spaces special appeal.

As you move away from Burnmoor Lodge, heading towards the eastern edge of the tarn, you reach an intersection of grassy pathways. Nearby, spanning Whillan Beck south-east of the tarn, stands Lambford Bridge. Head for this, and keep on along the path that swings across the lower slopes of Eskdale Fell, finally coming close to Eel Tarn. The tarn is not readily visible, sheltering behind a slight rise, but you can easily make out where it should be. Leave the path and find your way to the tarn which is one of the quietest and most relaxing spots in Lakeland, if you chose your day wisely.

Return eventually to the path and follow it, left (south-west), towards Boot. The path funnels you into the embrace of stone walls that guide you down from the moor. Through a gate a bridleway guides you back to Boot, easing down amid heavily-scented gorse bushes to emerge in the main street by the arched bridge.

TWA DOGS

This walk visits an outstanding viewpoint overlooking the market town of Keswick, but avoids the traditional steep climb by using an old railway.

DISTANCE:
5 miles (8 km)
WALKING
TIME: 3-4
hours
MAP: OS
Outdoor
Leisure Map 4
TERRAIN:
Easy, level
walking to
begin, with an
ascent to
Latrigg.
PARKING: Twa
Dogs, Keswick
(ask permission
first)

The original 18th-century inn was on the roadside, in front of the present building. This was demolished in 1966 and the present inn opened a year later. The name Twa Dogs comes from a poem of the same name by Robert Burns, probably written on one of his frequent visits to Keswick, where he paid his respects to the contemporary Lakeland poets. Today the inn prides itself on its traditional warmth and friendliness. Outside tables. Bar snacks menu available throughout the day. Children welcome, but no dogs inside the premises. Tel 017687 72599.

As you face the front of the Twa Dogs there is a small gate to the left which gives on to a narrow ginnel leading past the rear of houses to reach a flight of steps, on the left. This ascends to the trackbed of the Cockermouth, Keswick and Penrith Railway, which is now used for the Keswick Railway Footpath. Turn left along the track, which will speed you away from Keswick to the pleasant company of the River Greta and the

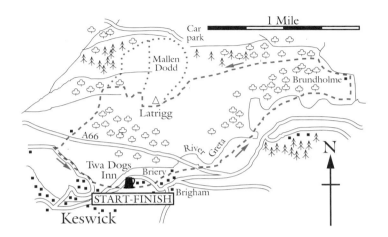

flanking confines of Brundholme Wood. The way forward could not be clearer, and once the path has passed beneath the A66 it reaches the site of a former bobbin mill at Lower Briery, from where bobbins were made and despatched to many parts of industrial northern England.

There is no hurry about the walk, as it flirts with the Greta through riverside meadows and woodlands that in springtime and early summer are bright with wild flowers. If you want a much shorter walk, just after an old railway bridge there is a permissive footpath descending left into Brundholme Wood which returns you to Keswick. Otherwise, press on steadily until you reach an old railway building on the right, now used as an information point. Near this go through a gate on the left, and cross a narrow neck of land to a back lane.

Turn left up the lane and ascend, a little steeply for a short while, swinging left past a modernised farm before climbing a little more to reach a footpath sign (Skiddaw and Underscar) on the right, at a wide gate (ignoring an earlier sign to Derwentfolds and Blencathra). Go through the gate on to a broad track swinging round a few gorse bushes, then running centrally up the eastern ridge of Latrigg. A short way on you encounter a plantation on the right. Keep going until, just before you reach the end of the plantation, you can climb left to the centre of the ridge to a stile. A short way on from the stile you promenade across the top of Latrigg.

Here there are stunning views of the Dodds, the central fells, the fells of the Newlands valley, the north west fells, and, to your right, the massive bulk of Skiddaw, Little

*Man and Lonscale Fell. If you pause and turn around you
will see Blencathra from an unfamiliar angle, one alas,
that fails to give a good impression of the mountain's
tumbling ridges.*

Just beyond the highest point of Latrigg, you will find a
bench from which to admire the view. From it a narrow
path descends steeply across the flank of the hill,
dropping down to intercept the Cumbria Way at one of a
number of possible points. Simply take the line which
best suits you, but it is a decision to be made higher
rather than lower down the fellside. If you feel
uncomfortable about this descent, which can be slippery
when wet, then simply backtrack a little and head east of
north from the highest point to reach the top of Gale
Road, near which you can turn left over a stile to return
to Keswick.

Once on the broad track that is the Cumbria Way and the
traditional line of ascent for Skiddaw, turn left, and
follow the track down to Spooney Green Lane, which
crosses the A66 dual carriageway and runs down to meet
a back lane at Briar Rigg. At this T-junction, turn left,
and follow the lane until you reach the former station, at
or near which you can rejoin the railway trackbed. This
will now shepherd you back to the point near the Twa
Dogs where you joined this rejuvenated footpath.

THE LANGSTRATH

In spite of an initially steep climb, this walk to Dock Tarn and Watendlath is not difficult, and rewards you with a stunning landscape at the very heart of Lakeland.

DISTANCE:
4 miles (7 km)
WALKING
TIME: 2^1/$_2$
hours
MAP: OS
Outdoor
Leisure Map 4
TERRAIN:
Rough and
rocky above the
valley, but
always on good
paths.
PARKING:
The Langstrath
Hotel (ask
permission first)

Originally built around 1590 as a miner's cottage, the Langstrath Hotel is secluded away in the unspoilt village of Stonethwaite, just off the main thrust of Borrowdale. The hotel is a small family run haven ideal for walkers and lovers of the countryside, and stands just a little aside from the popular Northern Coast to Coast walk and the Cumbria Way. Meals are served throughout the day up to 9.00pm. Children welcome, but no dogs, please. Tel 017687 77239.

Walk from the hotel back towards the village and as far as a red telephone box on the right. Turn right here to gain a pathway (signposted to Greenup Edge and Grasmere) leading down to a footbridge over Stonethwaite Beck. Once across the bridge and through a gate, turn right (signposted to Grasmere via Greenup Edge), walking roughly parallel with Stonethwaite Beck. After the second gate beyond Stonethwaite Bridge, locate a

path going left, slanting across a field and rising into a plantation.

The rising path crosses a wall before climbing through trees in a series of zigzags. It finally breaks free of the trees and out on to the heathered fell top. Follow the path, right, through two walls, and climb easily to reach Dock Tarn.

The tarn is set in a shallow basin with the great grassy mound of Ullscarf, regarded by many as the most central of Lakeland fells, away to your right. The reedy tarn, often populated by mallard, mirrors the sky and the surrounding hillsides and is an especially idyllic place to rest.

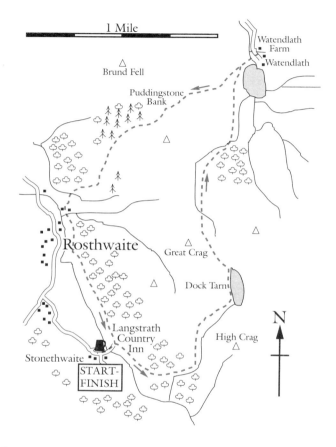

The continuing path keeps to the left (west) of Dock
Tarn, and passes through a brief rocky outcrop, before
setting off downhill on a paved pathway for the secluded
settlement of Watendlath. En route to Watendlath it
becomes possible (if time is short) to branch left and so

reach the bridleway linking Watendlath and Rosthwaite near to its highest point. But it is considerably more pleasurable to press on down all the way to Watendlath where you can buy refreshments. One of the cottages is said to be the home of Hugh Walpole's Judith Paris, a character in his Herries Chronicles.

To return from Watendlath simply retrace your steps over the beautiful single arch packhorse bridge, as if you were going back to Dock Tarn. But then follow the rising track on the right that guides you to the highest point at Puddingstone Bank, beyond which a gated track leads down towards Rosthwaite, reaching the valley near the Hazel Bank Hotel.

Rosthwaite is a small and peaceful community sitting beside the main Borrowdale road. Hugh Walpole unintentionally planted the seeds of discord here, for at least three cottages claim to be the setting for his Rogue Herries Farm.

At the Hazel Bank turn left on a track (signposted Stonethwaite and Watendlath) and follow this partly enclosed path as it runs alongside the beck and later becomes a field path with gates leading to Stonethwaite Bridge. At the highest point of the path Eagle Crag is especially prominent directly ahead, while away to the right you can pick out the summits of Base Brown, Green Gable and Lingmell, and the splendid waterfall of Taylorgill Force.

Turn right over Stonethwaite Bridge to retrace your outward steps to the Langstrath Hotel.

THE MILL INN

MUNGRISDALE

The grassy heights of Bannerdale Crags and Bowscale Fell receive only a modest share of attention. Yet the ascent of these outliers makes a fine undertaking.

DISTANCE: 7 miles (11.5km) WALKING TIME: 5 hours MAP: OS Outdoor Leisure Map 5 (except for a short section on Bowscale Fell) TERRAIN: Grassy, mainly with a discernible path. Not to be attempted in poor visibility. PARKING: The Mill Inn (ask permission).

To those who have been there, the relative anonymity of Mungrisdale is the secret of its charm. On the banks of the River Glenderamackin stands the 16th-century Mill Inn, resplendent with oak beams and an open fire. Over the centuries the inn has provided hospitality to such worthies as Charles Dickens and the legendary John Peel, who lies buried in Caldbeck churchyard only a few miles away. Bar meals from 12 noon-2pm and 6pm (6.30pm on Sundays)-9pm. Public bar closed on Sundays from 3-9.30pm. Children are welcome, as are dogs, but please leave dogs in the car or outside during meal times. Beer garden and outdoor seating. Tel 017687 79632.

Set off along the lane past the telephone box, and go through a gate on to a rough track heading towards a pyramidal shaped fell in front of you. This, known as The Tongue, is actually an elongated spur of Bowscale Fell. Beyond the gate the track dips slightly to cross a stream, following which you ascend on a clear track, climbing steadily

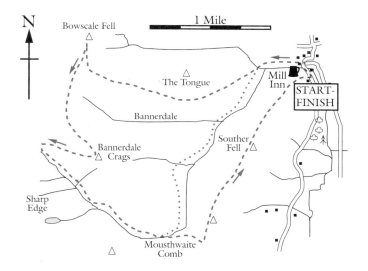

until the track forks at a small cairn. The track on the left is here the more prominent, and leads into Bannerdale, but ignore this and step up, right, to pursue a grassy ramp that rises in a straight line to the edge of the escarpment ahead.

On reaching the wide grassy col linking Bowscale Fell with Bannerdale Crags keep ahead until, at a small collapsed cairn, you reach a clear, grassy crosspath. Turn right here and stroll up to the stone shelter on the summit.

From the top of Bowscale Fell return to the crosspath, and go south, soon leaving the path and branching half left (south-east) to reach the Bannerdale escarpment. Take care here in winter because this edge, away from the prevailing wind, retains a large mass of snow and forms a series of cornices that must be avoided. But in summer you can safely follow the narrow path that runs along it, leading directly to the traditional summit of Bannerdale Crags, overlooking the dale below and Souther Fell. The true summit of Bannerdale lies a short distance further east, and provides a stunning prospect of the eastern slopes of Blencathra and Sharp Edge.

From the top of Bannerdale Crags the quickest way back is to return by your outward route, but otherwise head north-west and then west to reach the col north of Foule Crag and Blencathra. This can be a hit and miss experience in poor visibility with a long detour if your navigation is not one hundred percent.

Leave the col and descend south-

east on a path on the north side of the Glenderamackin which later drops towards the river past the remains of a former lead mine. Cross the river by a footbridge, and climb the opposite side to a neck of land known as White Horse Bent above Mousthwaite Comb. If you want to skip the ascent of Souther Fell do not cross the footbridge, but keep to the track above the Glenderamackin, to be led unerringly back to Mungrisdale.

From the col, head initially east and then north-east over trackless tussock grass to reach the higher ground of Souther Fell, and keep going to a cairn of large boulders on the highest point. Keep along the Souther Fell top, gradually and then steeply descending through bracken to reach Mungrisdale behind the Mill Inn.

SALUTATION INN

T H R E L K E L D

***P**eaceful rivers and becks, an old railway line and attractive farm fields and lanes all combine in this delightful circuit to the west of Threlkeld.*

DISTANCE:
4 miles (7 km)
WALKING
TIME: 2¹/₂ hours
MAP: OS
Outdoor Leisure
Map 4
TERRAIN:
Riverside paths,
old railway
trackbed and
country lanes.
PARKING: The
Salutation (no
need to ask
permission)

Tucked away in the quiet of Threlkeld, the 'Sally' is locally a popular inn, and one that walkers are getting to know. Its warm conviviality makes this a splendid launch pad for anyone exploring the ridges of Blencathra and the vast region known as Back o'Skiddaw. Bar meals are served every day (except Christmas Day) from 12 noon-2pm and 6.30-9pm. Children and dogs welcome. Tel 017687 79614.

Leave the car park at the Salutation and turn right, away from the village centre heading for the main A66 Keswick-Penrith road. When you reach it turn right and then cross it (with care), leaving it almost immediately down a country lane (signposted to Bridge End and Newsham) on the left.

Keep going to reach Mill Bridge which spans the River Glenderamackin, ignoring branching footpaths left and right of the bridge, but crossing the river. Turn right through a kissing gate and on to a

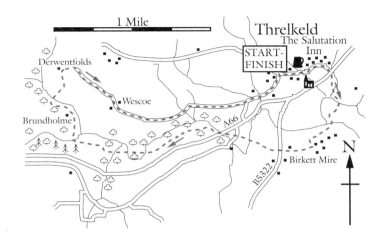

green path round a field margin on the left. The path gradually veers away from an adjoining fence after crossing a stream and keeps ahead to reach a rough access track over a stile. Turn right and walk on to reach the edge of a small caravan site near a farm. As you reach the farm, turn left to a gate. Cross the old railway line and walk up to another lane at a T-junction. Turn right and follow this lane until you reach a car park on the right just after the entrance to the Threlkeld depot workshop and store of the National Park.

Turn into the car park and locate a descending path at the rear, leading down steps to the B5322, St John's in the Vale road. Cross the road to a gate and climb to reach the trackbed of the former Cockermouth, Keswick and Penrith Railway, now part of the Keswick Railway

Footpath which is proving immensely popular both with pedestrians and cyclists.

Once on the old railway, which closed in 1972, keep going, wandering along pleasantly, and crossing the Glenderamackin again, before rising up steps to reach another quiet lane. Turn left and, after crossing Threlkeld Bridge and the Glenderamackin once more, leave the road on the right, through gates giving access to a path that runs beside the Glenderamackin and beneath the A66, to rejoin the old trackbed at a gate.

Turn left on to the trackbed and follow this extremely pleasant route for about a mile as it passes through Burns

Wood and Wescoe Wood until, just beyond a former railway building on the left now used as a small interpretive centre, you leave the trackbed on the right to cross a narrow neck of land to reach a lane.

Turn left up the lane, which climbs steepishly for a short while before levelling, with fine views ahead of Lonscale Fell. Rising again past a modernised farmhouse, the lane soon reaches a signposted path on the right (Derwentfolds and Blencathra), descending to cross Glenderaterra Beck by a footbridge. The path beyond rises easily up a sunken lane to reach another back lane at Derwentfolds, a charming group of cottages and farm buildings.

Turn right on the lane, which you now follow uneventfully, save for the need to evade the occasional vehicle and to take in the excellent views of the Dodds and the Helvellyn massif beyond, to reach Wescoe, a small settlement of farm buildings. Keep on through Wescoe, still on the road, resisting any temptation to take to signposted footpaths (which only lead into confusion amid countless farm fields). The lane eventually runs on to reach the road into Threlkeld, which takes you through this particularly delightful Lakeland village, back to the Salutation Inn.

BROTHERSWATER INN

Dovedale is a place you can instantly fall in love with. Indeed, one 18th-century writer described it as "a soft and delicate maiden".

DISTANCE: 7¹/₂ miles (12km)
WALKING TIME: 5 hours
MAP: OS Outdoor Leisure Map 5
TERRAIN: The most energetic walk in this book, with a fair amount of ascent. Good paths, but boots and other equipment are essential.
PARKING: Brotherswater Inn (ask permission first)

Now forming part of the Sykeside Camping Park, one of the finest sites in Lakeland with many amenities, the Brotherswater Inn caters for those who prefer a little more comfort. The inn is open every day of the year, serving snacks and bar meals during the day, and in the evening from 6-9.30pm. Dogs and children are welcome. Tel 017684 82239.

Wild and rugged are appropriate appellations to bestow on sylvan Dovedale for at its head rise the renowned precipices of Dove Crag on which routes were first pioneered as early as 1910. This round is a trek through the best of Dovedale, returning down delightful Caiston Glen.

From the inn set off into the campsite, following a broad track that leads to Hartsop Hall. Away to your right lies the broad expanse of Brothers Water, once known as Broad Water but renamed in memory of two brothers said to have drowned in its waters.

Hartsop Hall is a working farm,

dating from the 16th century, but extensively altered since then. It was formerly the home of the de Lancaster family, and later of Sir John Lowther who became the first Viscount Lonsdale at the end of the 17th century.

At Hartsop Hall you meet a signposted path heading left for Kirkstone Pass and Scandale. Ignore this (it is the way you will return), and keep right instead (signposted Dove Crag) on a good path rising steadily across the valley wall to a suspended cove beneath the precipices of Dove Crag.

To the right of the crag lies a gully of scree and projecting rocks. Ascend this, to reach a high, wide hollow containing a small tarn, with Dove Crag on your left and Hart Crag on your right. Keep climbing out of Houndshope Cove until you find a line of cairns leading to a collapsed wall across the stony col between Hart Crag and Dove Crag. Turn left and

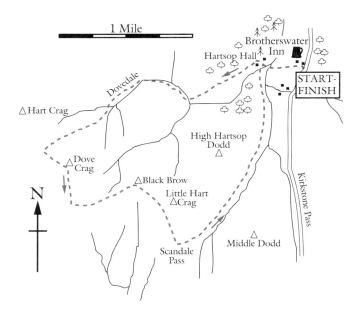

follow the wall to the top of Dove Crag.

The summit is not outstanding, but it commands an excellent view, obstructed only to the north-west by the bulk of Fairfield.

The remainder of the journey is virtually all downhill, and heads into a corner of Lakeland that is comparatively seldom visited. To begin, go south along the ridge, following the wall to a fenceline branching left at right angles. Turn along the fence (east) and on a path that drops steadily down grassy slopes. The going gets a little rougher before easing into the often boggy stretch known as Bakestones Moss.

Beyond Bakestones Moss lies Little Hart Crag, a double-topped fell in a splendid position at the head of Scandale. To reach Little Hart Crag, you must leave the path for a short while, and indulge in a little easy scrambling. The ongoing path thereafter maintains faith with the fenceline as it bends sharply, and runs down to Scandale Pass.

Rejoin the path and descend to Scandale Pass, turning left on a good path into Caiston Glen. Caiston Beck manages some attractive small waterfalls en route before it joins forces with Kirkstone Beck to flow into Brotherswater.

Cross Dovedale Beck and walk on through a clutch of gates to rejoin your outward route near Hartsop Hall, returning to Sykeside from there.

THE WHITE LION

PATTERDALE

A modest amount of pastoral lane walking is the price you pay for the marvellous landscapes of Boredale, one of Lakeland's hidden gems, and the Ullswater shore path.

DISTANCE: 8 miles (13km)
WALKING TIME: 4-5 hours
MAP: OS Outdoor Leisure Map 5
TERRAIN: Excellent paths throughout; some country lane walking.
PARKING: White Lion car park (ask permission first).

The distinctive 'narrowness' of the White Lion, perched bravely at the side of the road in Patterdale, is a unique feature both of the village and the valley. Visitors have been able to enjoy the hospitality of this historic country inn since the early 1800s, including William Wordsworth, who is said to have been in the bar when news arrived of the death of Nelson at Trafalgar. Walkers are most welcome here, the more the merrier. Children, too, and dogs. Bar meals are served from 12 noon-9.45pm, except Christmas Day. Tel 017684 82214.

Set off from the car park and turn right to a bend where you can stroll down a minor road leading to a group of cottages at Rooking. Follow the road to a gate, and turn right, through it, to gain a well-trodden path slanting across the lower slopes of Place Fell, a summit which by its proximity assumes monumental proportions. The path rises steadily to Boredale Hause, a long-established route across the fells. If the uphill work starts to get

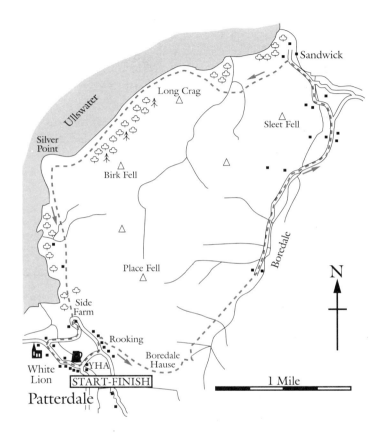

to you, the retrospective view across the valley, which takes in Striding Edge and Helvellyn, is a more than ample excuse to pause for a while.

As you reach Boredale Hause, move left on a gently-rising path that very soon forks. There is some potential for confusion here since paths also go left up Place Fell, and right across a stream to Angletarn Pikes. What you need to do is keep ahead, crossing the hause, west to east (the path soon becomes more evident), to reach a superb viewpoint at the top of a quite unexpected rocky gully, which lies at the head of the long valley of Boredale.

The fine ridge on your right as you look out from the top of the gully is that of Beda Fell, sandwiched between Boredale and the adjacent valley of Bannerdale. Descend the gully with care; there is a good path, but the upper section is a little loose. It does improve, however, as you go down into the valley, and the descent only requires a little thought over the placement of your feet.

The path slopes unerringly down to Boredale Head Farm, where you meet the valley road. This is a busy, working farm, but normally you can keep ahead through it. Occasionally if it is busy, you need to take to a permissive path that goes around the farm on the left. The road, which can be busy with visitors in summer months, then leads on in the company of Boredale Beck, which it later crosses at an ideal spot for a break.

Stay on the road to a branching road on the left leading down to Sandwick. Ignore another road (on the right) as you approach Doe Green Farm, and keep on around the grassy spur of Sleet Fell as far as a signpost on the left, pointing out the way back to Patterdale. Go left here, abandoning the road, following a good path near a wall.

Beyond Scalehow Beck (crossed by a footbridge) the path, providing intriguing glimpses of the lake, finally eases towards the Ullswater shoreline. Between Scalehow Beck and Silver Bay, the walking is of the very best, following a meandering path that joyously seems to go on forever. Just after a stretch of woodland, Silver Bay is reached, another perfect spot for a rest, and one you will find difficult to leave.

As you go round Silver Point, the path having toyed with meandering, now experiments with undulating, as a series of dips and cols tease you along the lake. Finally the path widens into a farm track, descending towards Side Farm. At Side Farm turn right between farm buildings and follow its access road out to the main valley road, to the George Starkey Memorial Hut. Turn left, to reach the White Lion in just a few minutes.

THE ROYAL HOTEL

D O C K R A Y

Gowbarrow will be forever associated with Wordsworth's poem about daffodils, which was inspired by Dorothy's mention of them in her journal in 1802.

DISTANCE: 8 miles (13km)
WALKING TIME: 4-4½ hours
MAP: OS Outdoor Leisure Map 5
TERRAIN: Excellent walking on good paths; a little on quiet lanes.
PARKING: Royal Hotel (ask permission first).

The Royal Hotel is a 16th-century coaching inn that enjoyed much trade with merchants travelling north and south across the Scottish border, which goes some way to explaining why you will find the Scottish coat of arms above the door. The interior has been completely refurbished in recent years, with a splendid flagged area, complete with leatherette-topped sewing machine tables, set aside for walkers. Bar meals are served all year from 12 noon-2.30pm and 6-9pm. Supervised children are welcome, but no dogs allowed inside the bar areas. Tel 017684 82356.

Aira Force is one of Lakeland's most endearing waterfalls, purchased with the landscaped land around by the National Trust in 1913. A visit to the waterfall is preceded by a splendid sweeping tour of Gowbarrow Fell, formerly a medieval deer park, and a visit to the cottages of Ulcat Row.

Leave the Royal Hotel and cross the main road to go down a lane opposite which takes you past Millses to a junction of pathways. The path

on your right is the way you will return, so, turn left through a gate. The ongoing path is quite delightful and changes direction as it negotiates the rocky base of Norman Crag at the north-western edge of Gowbarrow Fell. Now it heads north-east to meet a quiet country lane at a gate, not far from Ulcat Row.

The stretch of road walking that follows is extremely pleasant, and largely traffic free. Its inclusion is justified by the excuse it provides to visit Swinburn's Park. Turn right along the road to a T-junction. Turn right there to begin a short uphill pull to The Hause, a neat col beneath the slopes of Little Mell Fell.

Keep on down the road ignoring the lane to Dacre, and as you descend you see an escarpment, Priest's Crag, develop on the right. The route now lies across the base of the crag, and is reached by a gate beside the road. Beyond, the path rises gently to a col near Gate Crags, and immediately above Hagg Wood, it continues to climb through another gate, to go on below Little Meldrum. After rain the path is muddy especially where it contours round Great Meldrum and Kirksty Brow. Finally, at a wall, you re-enter National Trust property, near the ruins of a shooting lodge.

Walking south, climb a little to cross streams feeding Collierhagg Beck, and when the path divides, take the left

branch, undulating a little until you round a corner with the top of Yew Crag, a popular viewpoint, in sight below. Following the path, go down to a path junction near Lyulph's Tower, an 18th-century folly. Ignore a gate on your left, and bear right to another gate beyond, keeping left to a stile in a fence corner.

Soon after this you join the Aira Force path, which brings you out near the top of the falls. You will need to explore the obvious pathways to view the falls fully, so allow a little extra time for this because it is well worth it.

The whole area around Aira Force is very attractive; if you explore carefully you will find two stone bridges constructed in differing styles. The lower is built of vertical stones, not traditional in these parts, while the higher has horizontal stones, more in keeping with the vernacular. In spring and summer the woodlands are alive with birdlife, and brightly dotted with wild flowers. There are toilets down beside the car park if needed.

When you have finished exploring make your way back to the higher waterfall, High Force, where you will find a gate and a sign indicating a footpath to Dockray and Ulcat Row. Follow this through thinning woodland, until you find yourself back at the path junction near Millses, from where you can retrace your steps to the Royal.

PATTERDALE HOTEL

P A T T E R D A L E

his visit to Angletarn Pikes and their nearby tarn is one of the most delightful walks from Patterdale, and requiring only modest effort is within the capacity of everyone.

DISTANCE:
7¹/₂ miles
(12.5km)
WALKING
TIME: 4 hours
MAP: OS
Outdoor
Leisure Map 5
TERRAIN:
Good paths
throughout;
some fairly easy
uphill walking.
PARKING:
Patterdale Hotel
(ask permission
first)

The Patterdale Hotel has a long history in this popular valley, its convivial atmosphere and splendid accommodation providing a ready welcome to walkers whether staying only briefly or for a few days. Bar meals are served from 12 noon-2pm and from 6-8pm. Children are welcome, as are dogs, and there is a fine outdoor area in front of the hotel, with tables and chairs. Tel 017684 82231.

The walk to Angletarn Pikes is extended to include Hayeswater, beneath the slopes of High Street and Gray Crag, and a return through the charming village of Hartsop. The extension, however, is not compulsory, and you can simply wend your way back from Angletarn Pikes if you wish.

Leave the hotel car park and turn left, walking down the road to the George Starkey Memorial Hut on the right. Leave the road here, and go down a wide access leading to Side Farm, crossing Goldrill Beck on the way, a stream that was

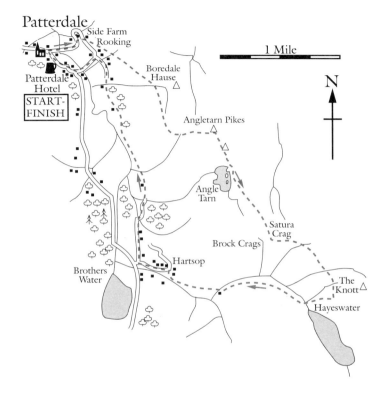

responsible for much of the alluvium that makes up the flat expanse of the dale at this point. Go between the buildings at Side Farm and turn right on to a broad track heading for the cottages at Rooking. At a gate turn left and go through another gate, in so doing reaching the steep, open flanks of Place Fell. Follow a path, trending right, to Boredale Hause. At a fork, take to the higher path to arrive at a conveniently-placed bench from which there is an outstanding view of the valley below.

The ongoing path now eases upwards to Boredale Hause, a flat, grassy col between hillocks, and from which a number of pathways radiate. On Boredale Hause are the ruins of what is thought to have been a small chapel, either serving the adjacent valleys or, more likely, as a place of worship (or shelter) for early travellers. Here also you find a couple of collapsed cairns, near which you move right across a small beck, ignoring all paths going off to the left. Across the beck, the path is never in doubt beginning a procession of twists and turns and ups and downs across grassy

knolls until, just as Angletarn Pikes come into view, there is an amazing view down to Brothers Water and the Kirkstone Pass, one of the finest viewpoints in Lakeland.

The path presses on easily, until you can leave it and scamper to the northernmost (and higher) top of Angletarn Pikes, crossing from there to a hollow to reach the southern top and its view of Angle Tarn. The tarn is a shapely stretch of water dotted with islands in a most idyllic setting, making this a suitable spot for lunch, and, on a quiet spring day very difficult to leave.

Go down towards the tarn, rejoining the main path left earlier, and follow it round Angle Tarn, climbing easily to a level section near Satura Crag. Go through a gate keeping below Satura Crag, and then cross a boggy patch as you deal with the weeping downflows of Prison Gill and Sulphury Gill.

Ahead now you can see the great grass-flanked hollow that contains Hayeswater, rising to a superb ring of fells including Gray Crag, Thornthwaite Crag, High Street, the Straits of Riggindale, and The Knott.

Beyond Sulphury Gill you encounter a path ascending from Hayeswater, and this should be followed down grassy slopes to the outflow, from where a broad track leads out of the valley. With time to spare you can use the ascending path to extend this walk to The Knott and Rampsgill Head, the latter providing an outstanding view into the rarely-seen sanctuary of Ramps Gill and upper Martindale. This extension would not add significantly to the walk, either in terms of time or distance. Retrace your steps to continue down to Hayeswater. Keep on through the car park at Hartsop, and ahead through the village until just before the main valley road you can turn right on a minor access road degenerating to a track. This takes a pleasant line along the base of the fells until, on reaching Rooking, you take a minor road on the left, back to Patterdale and the hotel.

THE BRIDGE HOTEL

B U T T E R M E R E

This simple tour of Buttermere is one of the most deservedly-popular short walks in Lakeland, suitable for any season.

DISTANCE: 4½ miles (7km)
WALKING TIME: 2-2½ hours
MAP: OS Outdoor Leisure Map 4
TERRAIN: Excellent paths and a little road walking.
PARKING: Bridge Hotel (ask permission first).

First licensed in 1735, the Bridge Hotel stands on a site that has been occupied for over 1,000 years, nestling between the twin lakes of Buttermere and Crummock Water and with the Buttermere fells surrounding it. The "bridge" is the old packhorse bridge in front of the hotel, over which Wordsworth, Ruskin and Southey first came to marvel at the area. There is excellent accommodation for walkers, and a very warm welcome. Bar meals are served every day from 12 noon-9.30pm. Children are welcome, but dogs should be confined to the patio area. Tel 017687 70252.

Leave the hotel and go to the left of the nearby Fish Hotel to follow a broad track through gates (ignore the deviation to Scale Force) until, as you approach the water's edge, you can pursue a hedgerow down to a bridge at Buttermere Dubs. There is an especially fine view from here down the length of the lake to the brooding form of Fleetwith Pike at the head of the dale.

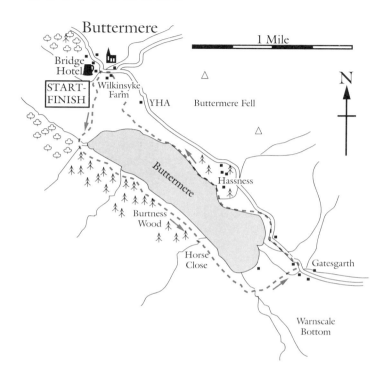

Cross the bridge and a small footbridge nearby, to go through a gate in a wall at the foot of Burtness Wood. Turn left on a track through the woodland that roughly follows the shoreline of the lake, finally emerging from Burtness Wood near Horse Close, where a bridge spans Comb Beck. Keep on along the path until you reach a wall guiding you to a sheepfold and a gate. Go left through the gate, cross Warnscale Beck and press on to Gatescarth Farm. At the farm take the gate marked

'Lakeside Path', and follow signs to reach the valley road. (NOTE: There may be some footpath realignment in this area during 1997, which may affect these instructions slightly.)

A short stretch of road walking, left on the B5289, now follows, along which there are no pathways, but when the road bends right, leave it for a footpath on the left (signposted Buttermere via Lakeshore Path). The path brings you to a step stile into a field. The path never strays far from the shoreline and leads to a stand of Scots pine, near Crag Wood.

Beyond Hassnesshow Beck, the path enters the grounds of

Hassness, where a rocky path, enclosed by trees, leads to a kissing gate. Here a path has been cut into the crag, where it plunges into the lake below, and the path disappears into a tunnel. This was cut by employees of George Benson, a 19th-century Manchester mill owner who then owned the Hassness Estate, so that he could walk around the lake without straying too far from its shore.

After the tunnel (closed in 1996 following a roof collapse, when a diversion was introduced) a gate gives access to a gravel path through a wooded pasture, beyond which you can turn right on a fenced path that crosses a traditional Lakeland bridge of slate slabs. A short way on, through another gate, a path leads you on to Wilkinsyke Farm, and an easy walk out to the road, just a short way above the Bridge Hotel.

THE FISH HOTEL

B U T T E R M E R E

A visit to one of Lakeland's most renowned waterfalls is the reward for a modest expenditure of energy on this brief walk to Scale Force.

DISTANCE:
4 miles (6.5km)
WALKING
TIME: 2 hours
MAP: OS
Outdoor Leisure
Map 4
TERRAIN:
Easy walking on
good paths.
PARKING:
Use the
National Park
car park (pay
and display)
adjoining the
hotel.

The Fish Hotel is especially renowned in tales of old Lakeland for the story of Mary Robinson, the so-called Maid of Buttermere, who lived and worked at the hotel. Her story was brought to fame following a visit by Captain Budworth at the turn of the 18th century. She was later wooed by, and eventually married, John Hadfield, who turned out to be an imposter and who was later hanged at Carlisle for forgery. The tale is evocatively told in Melvyn Bragg's *Maid of Buttermere*. The hotel today is at the centre of a popular walking area, and caters well for walkers. It is bright and cheerful, and you can be sure of a warm welcome. Bar meals are served every day (except Christmas Day) from 12 noon-2pm and 6-9pm. Children are most welcome, but because the hotel is fully used for catering, dogs cannot be taken inside. Tel 017687 70253.

From the car park walk round in front of the hotel and go down a lane on the other side that leads to a gate on the right (signposted Scale Bridge, Scale Force). Follow this path to Buttermere Dubs – a dub being a pool in a river, here linking the two lakes. Cross Scales Bridge, an attractive twin-arched stone construction, typical of many you will find in the Lake District.

Turn right and follow a path first crossing Near and then Far Ruddy Becks. Stay with the gently rising path, following a line of cairns to reach a large cairn near a group of holly trees. Bear left, still following cairns, later trending slightly to the right as the stony path keeps on below a line of hawthorns. The continuing path crosses a small stream before heading for a gap in a wall beyond which it drops to the bridge immediately below Scale Force.

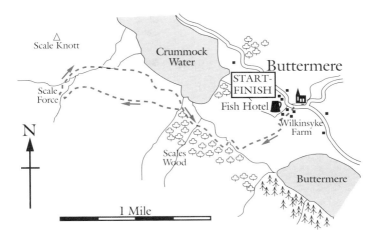

Scale Force is the highest waterfall in Lakeland, at its most sensational following prolonged rain. It is 125 feet (38 metres) high, and leans back shyly in a tree-lined cleft into which you need to scramble to get a better view, but take care on the slippery rocks.

If you wish, you can return the same way, but you can add a little extra by following a path going down with the stream flowing from the Force, towards Crummock Water. Cross Black Beck by a bridge, and go past the barely-noticeable remains of an early settlement, probably founded on iron smelting.

After a sheepfold, turn right across another bridge on to a bracken-flanked pathway heading for a group of trees and shortly afterwards a rectangular-looking boulder. Keep ahead in the same direction and soon you will find yourself back on the path you used on your outward journey. Simply follow this back to the Fish Hotel.

THE TRAVELLERS REST

GRASMERE

*W*aterfalls
and a dark
tarn nestling
in a vast
grassy hollow
are the
reward for
this simple
walk from the
outskirts of
Grasmere.

DISTANCE:
4¹/₂ miles
(7.5km)
WALKING
TIME:
2¹/₂ hours
MAP: OS
Outdoor
Leisure Map 5
TERRAIN:
Good paths
throughout.
PARKING:
Travellers Rest
(ask permission
first – see
notice in car
park).

Full of old world charm and
character with oak beams and
inglenooks, the Travellers Rest,
formerly a 16th-century coaching
inn, epitomises the traditional Lake
District hostelry. Roaring log fires in
winter and beer gardens with
panoramic views for warm summer
days are features walkers will enjoy.
Children, for whom there is an
outdoor play area in summer, and
dogs, are welcome. Bar meals are
served from Easter-October from 12
noon-9.45pm, and the rest of the
year from 12 noon-3pm and 6-
9.30pm. Tel 015394 35604.

*This short walk to Grisedale Tarn,
sandwiched between the massifs of
Fairfield and Helvellyn, is a delight at
any time of the year, though it may be
a little tricky in winter conditions.*

Leave the car park and turn right up
the main road to a left bend. Here,
on the right, you can join the
Northern Coast to Coast Walk, at
this point a bridleway (signposted
Patterdale) running beside attractive
cottages. The bridleway becomes
flanked by walls and climbs steadily

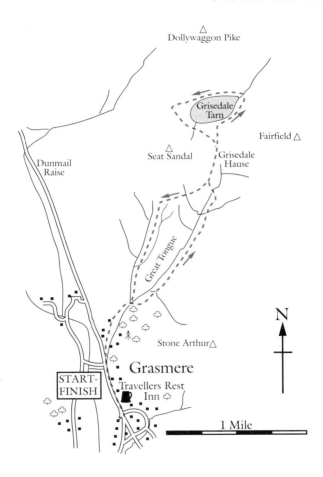

to a gate. Beyond the gate, keep climbing for a while until the path levels near a group of sheep enclosures at the very tip of Great Tongue. Turn right first to cross Little Tongue Gill and then Tongue Gill, thereafter rise in easy stages on a good path across the lower flanks of Great Rigg. The retrospective view from the path is always good and improves with height, so you have ample excuse to pause for a breather.

Gradually you approach waterfalls at the head of the gill, where you also encounter the barrier of a rock step that is surmounted easily enough using a series of ledges and a rough path that crosses them. The path then runs on a little to cross a feeder stream of the gill, beyond which you turn right, climbing rough ground to a false col on the edge of a shallow hollow. Keep this on your right, and ascend easily to Grisedale Hause, beyond which your objective, Grisedale Tarn, awaits.

There is a legend that Duvenald (corrupted to Dunmail),

King of Strathclyde, whose kingdom then embraced this part of north Cumbria, cast his crown and insignia of office into the tarn before setting off on a pilgrimage. Other tales suggest he lies buried beneath the large cairn at the top of Dunmail Raise, having been slain by Saxons. Fact, as ever, has a nasty habit of destroying such legends, for the king died peacefully in his bed in Rome.

From the hause, go ahead on the prominent path, keeping Grisedale Tarn on your left. You cross the outflow easily enough, and can circle all the way round the tarn on one or more paths, some stretches of which can be wet. In doing so you return to Grisedale Hause, so this circuit is an optional extra – you may just decide to sit among the rocks near the outflow, contemplating the beautiful setting.

On returning to Grisedale Hause, start retracing your steps, but do not cross the stream to reach the waterfalls. Instead, keep slightly to the right, this time descending by way of Little Tongue Gill, which was the way the Victorians came on ponies as they ascended Helvellyn. The path, for the most part grassy, slips steadily downwards to rejoin the outward route near the foot of the Tongue. From there retrace your steps to the Travellers Rest.

THE LAMB INN

G R A S M E R E

Concealed among the flowing folds of fells known as Grasmere Common, Easedale Tarn and Codale Tarn have been places of popular pilgrimage since Victorian times.

DISTANCE: 8¾ miles (14km)
WALKING TIME: 5 hours
MAP: OS Outdoor Leisure Map 6
TERRAIN: Generally on good paths, not suitable in mist.
PARKING: The Lamb Inn (ask permission first).

The bar at the Lamb Inn welcomes walkers, children and dogs. The Inn forms part of the Red Lion Hotel, which is able to provide accommodation for those wanting to stay over in Grasmere, one of the most popular Lakeland honeypots. Bar meals are served every day from 12 noon-2.30pm and 6.30-9.00pm. Tel 015394 35456.

To the north-east of Grasmere, across the valley of Far Easedale, lies Helm Crag, its topmost rocks long since christened "the Lion and the Lamb", an attribute best observed from the main valley road. When you are standing next to them no amount of head scratching can fathom why.

This circular walk embraces both Easedale and Codale Tarn, with the option of continuing along a fine ridge to reach Helm Crag. It climbs out of Easedale on to the delightful Blea Rigg and crosses to Sergeant Man, before returning to the head of Far Easedale.

The way out of Grasmere lies up Easedale Road, reached from the

Lamb Inn by following the road towards the village centre. Turn left up Easedale Road, heading towards Goody Bridge.

Occasionally you can escape the attentions of passing cars by taking to a roadside path, but this is not always possible, so take care. Keep going until you arrive at a footpath (signposted to Easedale Tarn), just at a bend. Cross Easedale Beck and continue towards the conspicuous white splash of Sourmilk Gill which you can see ahead. The path rises with the gill and turns abruptly left round Brinhowe Crag as you reach the head of the falls, before continuing uneventfully to Easedale Tarn. This splendid oasis is set among bracken- and grass-clad hummocks punctuated by small rocky outcrops and the pyramidal form of Belles Knott.

Moving on, another climb takes you up between Eagle Crag and Belles Knott, where the path forks. The right

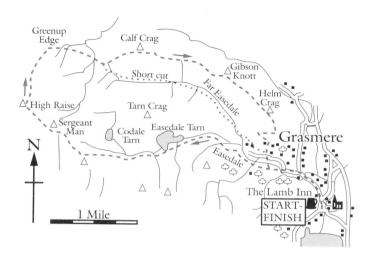

branch visits Codale Tarn, a worthwhile diversion, from where you may decide to retrace your steps to Grasmere.

The continuing route rises by the left branch, climbing steadily until suddenly the vast bowl containing Stickle Tarn lies dramatically at your feet.

Looking back down into Easedale the landscape of rolling fells and dark tarns backed by the swelling heights of Fairfield and the Helvellyn range is the kind of vision of loveliness that brings walkers back to the Lake District time and time again.

The path now sets off easily, north-west to Sergeant Man, skirting this delightful vantage point. Beyond, a grassy track leads to the slightly higher plateau (boggy after rain) of High Raise, then descending slightly to reach Low White Stones.

Heading north-north-east, the path goes easily down to the boggy and potentially confusing col of Greenup Edge, where it meets the Northern Coast to Coast Walk, pioneered by Alfred Wainwright. From the col a path descends across a boggy shelf at the head of Wyth Burn, running on to a broad col at the head of Far Easedale.

Here you have a choice. Either descend the obvious bridleway going south of east to rejoin the road back to Grasmere. Or you can ignore the path and branch slightly left to take a prominent, narrow path that goes round Calf Crag and on to Gibson Knott. The path rarely sticks to the crest of the ridge, preferring to cast about from side to side. Eventually it crosses a dip to Bracken Hause before concluding with a rocky flourish to gain the jumbled chaos of Helm Crag. Many of the crags that adorn the top of Helm Crag have been given names, including the highest point itself, which for obvious reasons is called the Howitzer.

As you leave the summit, you descend to the extreme edge of the ridge to a steep slope, and an engineered path that zigzags to the valley bottom. Take care on this descent especially if the rocks are wet. A simple stroll back along Easedale Road is all that then remains.

TOWER BANK ARMS

N E A R S A W R E Y

__B__eatrix Potter's Hill Top is a magnet that causes long traffic jams in summer. This splendid walk over adjacent Claife Heights is one you can do at any time.

DISTANCE: 4½ miles (7.5km)

WALKING TIME: 3-3½ hours

MAP: OS Outdoor Leisure Map 7

TERRAIN: Good, but with some awkward going in the woodland of Claife Heights.

PARKING: NT car park for Hill Top also serves the Tower Bank Arms. Avoid parking on the road.

Well frequented by visitors to Hill Top, the Tower Bank Arms is an apparently innocuous pub set at an angle to the road, but its low beamed main bar with high-backed settles on a rough floor gives it a unique and homely character. Children are welcome at lunchtime only, as are well-behaved dogs. Bar meals are served every day except Christmas Day from 12 noon to 2pm, and 6.30-9pm. Tel 015394 36334.

Leave the car park and turn right up the road for a few strides and then take the first turning on the left to a farm at the lane end. Keep going through the buildings to reach a broad gravel track. At the next set of farm buildings take the left-hand of two gates (stile), continuing on a gravel track once more.

Before long the path skirts Moss Eccles Tarn, a splendid place to rest for a while, set against a backdrop of the central Lakeland fells among which the Langdale Pikes are especially prominent. The path continues uneventfully past more

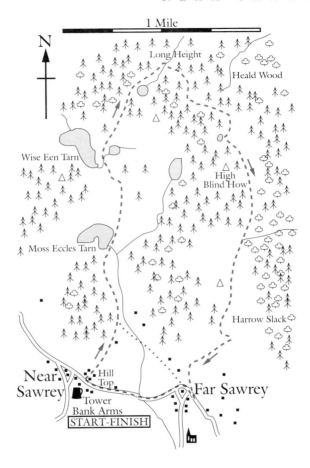

tarns, including Wise Een Tarn, to enter a large plantation at a gate. A short way in ignore a branching bridleway on the left and stay on the main track which swings to the right and descends.

Part way down at a bend swinging left you encounter a signpost (Hawkshead Ferry and Far Sawrey) on the right. Leave the main track here for a footpath into the plantation, which can be slippery after rain. The way on is waymarked by posts topped with white paint, and these serve to guide you well through the trees to the highest point of Claife Heights where a few highly-polished rocks provide a splendid perch from which to look out over Windermere to Wansfell Pike and the distant fells of the Kentmere Horseshoe.

The path continues across Claife Heights, descending now and never in doubt. It emerges at a broad forest trail. Turn right along the trail for a short distance, and then leave it on the left. The footpath finally descends to meet a bridleway. Turn right here (signposted Far Sawrey), through a gate, and follow the track through relaxing scenery to reach the valley road at Far Sawrey.

Turn right along the road, but do take care against speeding traffic on this narrow country lane. Once clear of Far Sawrey, look for a signposted footpath on the left, behind a hedgerow. This will allow you to progress rather more safely towards Near Sawrey, finally emerging on to the road again just above the village.

As an alternative finish, you can follow the road through Far Sawrey for a short distance, as far as a public bridleway on the right (signposted to Moss Eccles Tarn and Claife Heights) and use this to rise easily to meet the path used on the outward section of the walk. Turn left to return to Near Sawrey.

KINGS ARMS HOTEL

HAWKSHEAD

A splendid panorama is the reward for anyone who climbs Latterbarrow. This approach uses an old bridleway that crosses the northern slopes of Claife Heights.

DISTANCE:
3¹/₂ miles
(6km)
WALKING
TIME: 2 hours
MAP: OS
Outdoor
Leisure Map 7
TERRAIN:
Good paths
throughout,
but a little
confusing in
the plantations.
PARKING:
Village car park.
Permits
available from
the Kings Arms.

In summer it is a particular delight to sit outside the Kings Arms on the terrace overlooking the square in this Tudor village. Spring and autumn, however, are better times to go in search of a modicum of peace and tranquillity; and winter, too, has its attractions. Bar meals are served from 12 noon-2.30pm and 6-9pm. Children and dogs are welcome. Tel 015394 36372.

Leave the village car park at its southern edge, turning left on to the Sawrey road until, at the first junction, you can branch left on a narrow lane (signposted to Wray and Wray Castle). Follow this lane into the hamlet of Colthouse, continuing northwards for about 250 yards beyond the last buildings to a bridleway on the right.

Leave the road here, turning acutely right, through a gate on a rising track.

The track now continues for quite some distance as it lopes across the northern slopes of Claife Heights, for the most part in and out of mixed woodland for a little over a mile. At a gate, by which time you are convinced you have gone too far, turn left (signposted to Latterbarrow) following a line of posts topped with white paint that take you downhill for a short distance, then bending left and climbing to begin a more or less level passage through the trees.

Not until the last moment does it become apparent that the grassy dome of Latterbarrow is there at all,

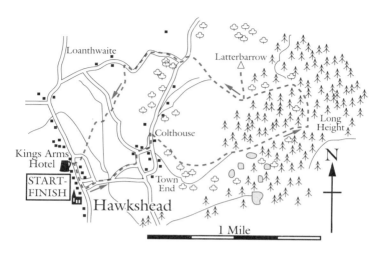

always being shielded by trees. Progress through the trees, however, is never as dismal as some forests can be, and in spring especially there is plenty of opportunity to hear and identify woodland birds.

Eventually, the track runs out of the trees, and continues for a short distance to a waymark/signpost at a fence corner (stile). Over the stile one path descends to Hawkshead, the other ascends to Latterbarrow. Go right to Latterbarrow on a steadily rising track that leads directly to the enormous monument crowning the summit. As a viewpoint, the top of Latterbarrow is as good as many in Lakeland, especially so northwards across Ambleside at the head of Windermere and the ring of summits flanking Fairfield.

From the summit you can either retrace your steps to the

signpost, turning right to begin the descent to Hawkshead, or you can use a more direct line from the top of the fell. Either way the two paths combine, and lead down to a country lane. Turn left for about 50m/yds and then right on to Loanthwaite Lane, where care is needed because of the occasional vehicle that passes this way. After a little under half a mile look for the second signposted footpath on the left, and use this to follow a waymarked route pleasantly through meadows to reach Scar House Lane. Turn left along the lane, and very soon right into another meadow, with Hawkshead now plainly visible ahead. The continuing path shepherds you unerringly back to Hawkshead.

As you reach a road, cross it, continuing ahead past attractive cottages and through an archway to arrive at the rear of the Kings Arms Hotel in the square, which is entered via an archway.

MORTAL MAN

T R O U T B E C K

The Mortal Man is flanked by some of Lakeland's best scenery, lying beneath the western arm of the famous Kentmere Horseshoe walk. The inn has long been popular and stands beside the old coaching route between Ambleside and Patterdale. The bar, warmed in winter by a roaring fire, is a friendly arrangement of farmhouse chairs around copper-topped tables. Dogs and children are welcome. Bar meals served every day from 12 noon to 1.50pm, and during evenings (Monday excepted) from 6.30-9pm. Tel 015394 33193.

Walk away from the Mortal Man slightly downhill on a surfaced lane which starts to climb as a rough track. Keep going up this, and when the track emerges close by the main Troutbeck road swing to the right and follow a descending track past High Green Lodge.

The track brings you out on the main road to Kirkstone, and on reaching it turn right for a short distance to a signposted bridleway on the left, opposite a minor road

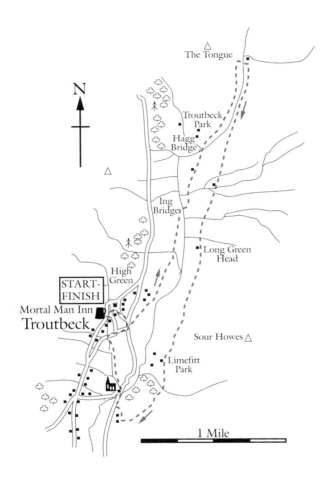

junction. Turn down beside a wall, and at the bottom of
the bridleway turn right on meeting surfaced Ing Lane
and follow it to Ing Bridge, which spans Trout Beck.

Press on along the lane as far as Hagg Bridge, which is not especially prominent. It spans Hagg Gill near its confluence with Trout Beck. Here the lane bends slightly left to go up to Troutbeck Park, but you should leave it near an ash tree, heading roughly in line with Hagg Gill for two dead trees ahead and to the right of Hall Hill, a small grassy mound. The footpath on the ground is not clear, but your objective is a gap in the intake wall above. When you reach the gap pause for a moment to admire the view down the length of this stunning valley before turning right along a rough track that rises slightly and curves round to meet a gate. Keep going to a second gate at which you can turn sharply right through another gate, descending to cross Hagg Gill near a barn. Once

across the gill, head briefly towards a small section of quarry spoil, soon leaving a broad track for a narrower path running to the right below the quarry, and quickly leaving it behind.

The way forward is now not in doubt, passing in easy fashion along the very base of the Kentmere summits, notably Yoke and Sallows, for a little over 2 miles (3km) until you are above Limefitt Caravan and Camping Park. Where the path forks, branch left, ascending gently and in due course along a line of hawthorns to meet the Garburn Road, a long-established pass linking the valley of Troutbeck with Kentmere and Longsleddale beyond.

Turn right on Garburn Road and in a few strides branch right again, continuing pleasantly down to reach the main road. Turn right, and cross Trout Beck once more, until, just past the church, you can leave the road for a bridleway on the left. Ignore a public footpath on the right, and keep on to cross a stream, turning right immediately on crossing the stream to go up to a gate. Through the gate, turn left and ascend a green path beside a wall to another gate giving access to a walled pathway, which closes down to a hedgerowed path that leads up to a crossing track. Turn right along this just below cottages, and keep going to reach a surfaced lane at a bend. Turn left with the Mortal Man up above you on the left, and follow the lane back to the starting point.

THE WATERMILL

An ideal opportunity to explore a charming area often overlooked by motorised walkers heading for Windermere and the fells of central Lakeland.

DISTANCE: 4¹/₄ miles (7.5 km)
WALKING TIME: 2¹/₂ hours
MAP: OS Outdoor Leisure Map 7
TERRAIN: Generally on lanes and good, but occasionally indistinct paths.
PARKING: The Watermill (ask permission)

In an ideal location for touring the Lakes, the Watermill is situated in a quiet backwater, east of Windermere. Formerly a wood mill, the Watermill has been converted into a traditional inn full of character and atmosphere yet still retaining many features of its past when it crafted cart wheels, shuttles and bobbins for the Lancashire cotton mills. Machinery was powered by a water wheel via a mill race in the River Gowan, which flows through the grounds. The inn is a free house serving up to 14 traditional ales, and bar meals every day from 12 noon-2pm and 6.15-9pm. Walkers are asked to use the public bar. Children are welcome in the lounge, and dogs in the bar. Tel 01539 821309.

Leave the Watermill and turn right as if walking out to the main road. In a short distance, turn left on a quiet lane that runs on to pass beneath the railway, before bending sharply right, and then easing round to the left. You leave the lane for a green bridleway (signposted) on the right (not a footpath, which is encountered earlier), running beside a wall. A short way on the bridleway moves away from the wall and heads towards a gate giving access to a small woodland, which contains extensive banks of wood sorrel.

You leave the woodland at another gate, continuing ahead beside a wall. Keep on towards Whasdike Farm where you meet a surfaced lane. Go left along the lane and at a junction branch right, down to a gate, after which you leave the track to the left, heading to the right of a tin-roofed shed, beyond which you can pick out a waymark on a small rise. From the waymark, locate another waymark that guides you into and through Schoolknott Plantation.

Emerging from the plantation keep generally ahead for some distance. There are a number of potentially confusing trackways

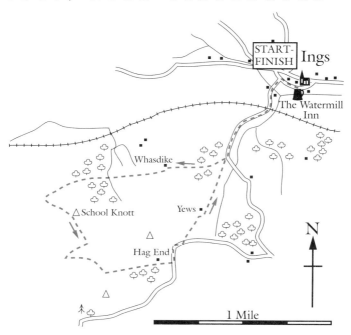

along this section, but if you keep going forward you will pass a gate on the right to reach a second gate near a sycamore tree. Branch left here on a rising grassy path that takes you over the rise of School Knott, beyond which you can descend easily to a gate close by a small tarn. Through the gate, keep the tarn on your left and follow a path round to the right and then ahead for about 250 m/yds to a gate on the left where you meet the Dales Way, a splendid 88-mile walk from Ilkley in the Yorkshire Dales to Bowness-on-Windermere.

Go left through the gate, where you will see the Dales

Way rising as a rough track. Follow this for a short while diagonally left to a wall corner, then ahead and left to cross through another wall, after which the path is more evident and guides you out to Hag End Farm. Go into and through the farmyard, leaving along its access to reach a back lane. At the lane turn left, following the lane round for about 200m/yds to a footpath on the left. Cross a rough meadow to a fence and stile. Over the stile turn right along the fenceline until you meet a more obvious track bearing left to a through-stile over a short section of wall, and then head down to join a surfaced access road.

Keep ahead, across the road, towards Yews to reach a ladder stile on the right, and then go down the next field (no clear pathway), through a gated gap, then bearing slightly left to reach another stile near a tree. Once over this stile you soon reach the lane along which you started the walk, about 100m/yds away from the point at which you left it. Now simply turn left on the lane and retrace your steps to Ings.